Disney **LEARNING**

ENGLISH
BRAIN BOOST

GRADE
**1**

**NELSON**

This workbook belongs to:

_____

Disney LEARNING

Published by Nelson Education Ltd.

ISBN-13: 978-0-17-685496-6
ISBN-10: 0-17-685496-7

Printed and bound in Canada
1 2 3 4   21 20 19 18

For more information contact Nelson Education Ltd.,
1120 Birchmount Road, Toronto, Ontario  M1K 5G4.
Or you can visit our website at nelson.com.

# Contents

| | |
|---|---|
| Track Your Learning | 2 |
| Alphabet Knowledge | 4 |
| Word Knowledge | 29 |
| Comprehension | 62 |
| Writing and Grammar | 84 |
| Answers | 100 |
| Flash Cards | 111 |
| Completion Certificate | 117 |

# Track Your Learning

START | 1 | 2 | 3 | 4 | 5

25 | 24 | 23 | 22 | 21 | 20 | 19 | 18

26 | 27 | 28 | 29 | 30 | 31 | 32

53 | 52 | 51 | 50 | 49 | 48 | 47

54 | 55 | 56 | 57 | 58

79 | 78 | 77 | 76 | 75 | 74 | 73

80 | 81 | 82 | 83 | 84 | 85

Colour a circle for every completed activity to finish the Brain Boost learning path!

6 · 7 · 8 · 9 · 10 · 11

17 · 16 · 15 · 14 · 13 · 12

33 · 34 · 35 · 36 · 37 · 38 · 39

46 · 45 · 44 · 43 · 42 · 41 · 40

59 · 60 · 61 · 62 · 63 · 64

72 · 71 · 70 · 69 · 68 · 67 · 66 · 65

86 · 87 · 88 · 89 · FINISH

# Matching

What sea animals live near Ariel?
Draw a line from each letter to the
picture that begins with that letter.

f

d

w

s

# Solve the Riddles

Where does Ariel live? Solve the riddles. Then complete the mystery word to find out!

1. I am curved.

   The word **sun** starts with me.

   What letter am I? ____
                                    1

2. I am in the word **bee**.

   In fact, there are two of me.

   What letter am I? ____
                                    2

3. I am the first letter in the alphabet!

   The word **apple** starts with me.

   What letter am I? ____
                                    3

Mystery Word: ____ ____ ____
                           1     2     3

# Colour to Complete

Dory finds a clue. What does she find? To find out, colour the picture. Use the Colour Key.

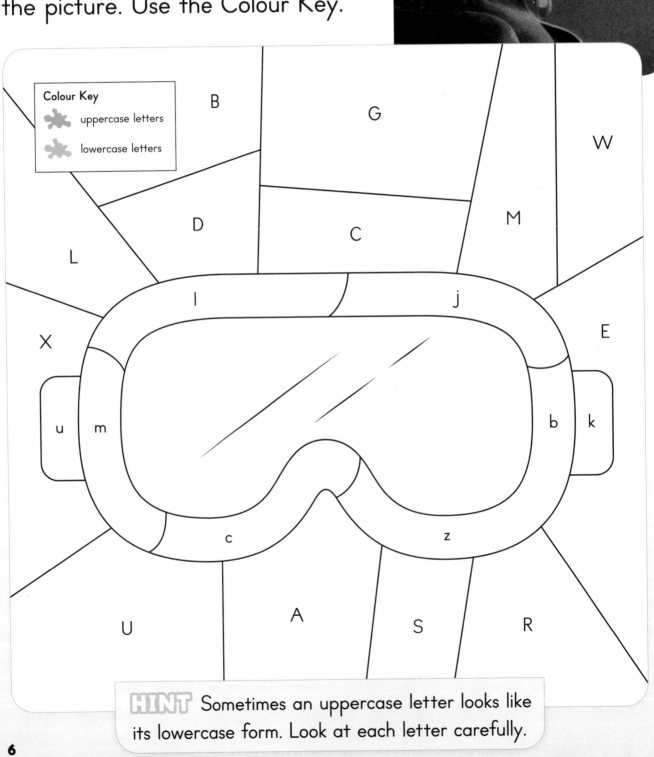

**Colour Key**

uppercase letters

lowercase letters

**HINT** Sometimes an uppercase letter looks like its lowercase form. Look at each letter carefully.

# Matching

Many sea creatures hear about Marlin and Dory's adventure. Who are they? Draw a line from each letter on the left to the sea creature that begins with that letter.

l

d

f

s

# Fill In the Blanks

Trace each missing letter. Read the story.

Ariel swims in the sea.

She swims with Flounder.

They see two whales.

The whales are happy.

Ariel and Flounder are happy too.

# Unscramble the Words

Ariel and Flounder find lots of treasure in the sea! Unscramble the letters to form words.

**btoo**

_____

**frko**

_____

**jgu**

_____

**HINT** The first letter in each word is in the correct spot.

# Puzzle Pieces

Nemo is exploring. What might he find? Trace the letter in each puzzle piece. Then write each word on the line.

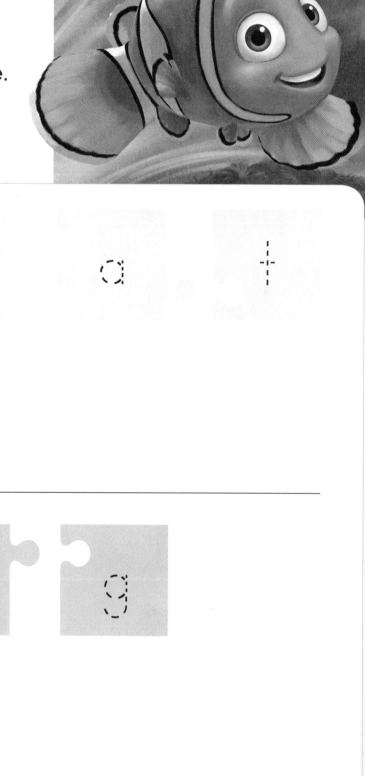

b          o          a          t

_____

l       o       g

_____

# Fill In the Blanks

Trace each missing letter. Read the story.

Nemo is going to school.

Nemo likes school.

He sees his friends there.

He learns at school.

Nemo has lots of fun.

# Maze

Ariel needs to find her way to Eric's ship. Follow the lowercase letters through the maze.

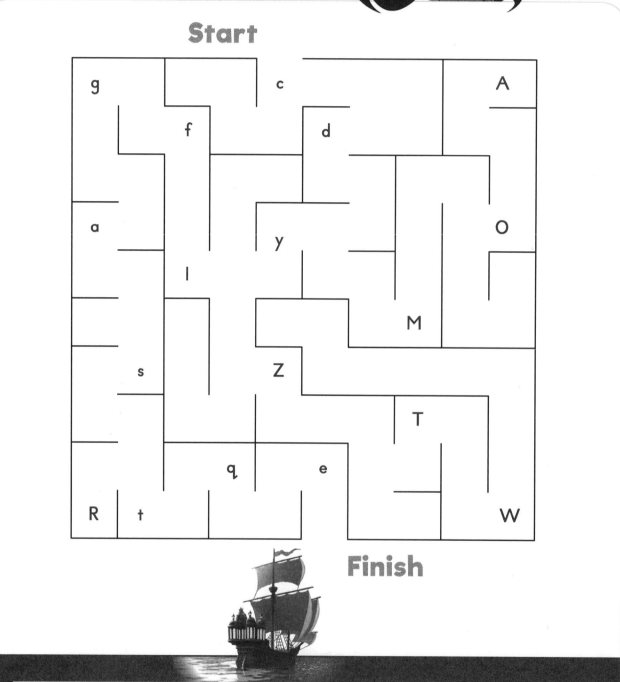

**HINT** Look carefully at each letter. Compare the size of letters.

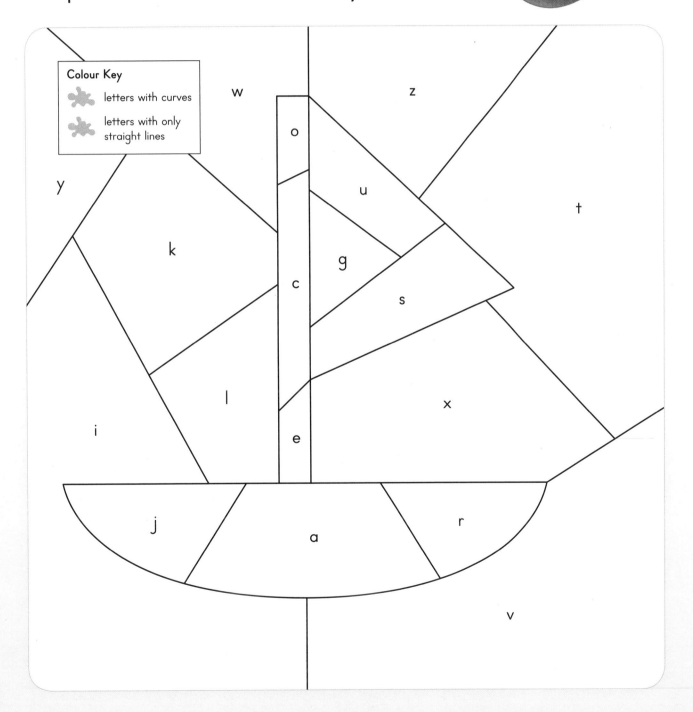

# Colour to Complete

Where does Ariel find her treasures? To find out, colour the picture. Use the Colour Key.

**Colour Key**

letters with curves

letters with only straight lines

w

z

o

y

u

t

k

g

c

s

l

x

i

e

j

a

r

v

# Matching

These red fish match! Match each uppercase letter with the correct lowercase letter.

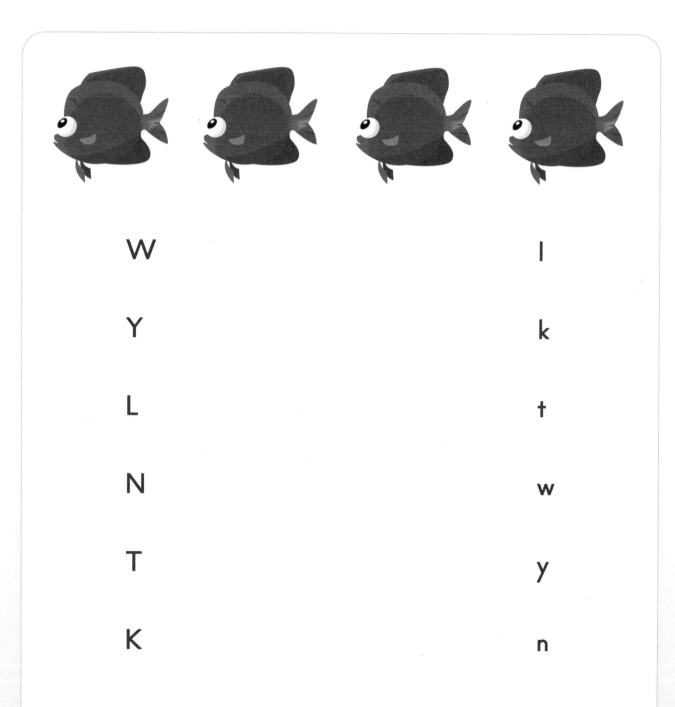

| | |
|---|---|
| W | l |
| Y | k |
| L | t |
| N | w |
| T | y |
| K | n |

# Puzzle Pieces

Some fish are small. Some fish are big. Letters come in different sizes too. Match the uppercase and lowercase letters in the puzzle pieces.

h

f

K

Z

z

H

F

k

# Connect the Dots

Find out what Scuttle is holding. Connect the dots in alphabetical order.

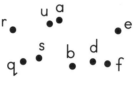

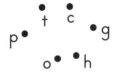

**HINT** Start at **a** and then draw a line to **b**.

16

# Maze

Eric's dog, Max, is missing. Follow the letters in alphabetical order to lead Eric to Max.

**Start**

**Finish**

# Out of Order

Bruce chases Dory. Fix each sentence.
Put the words in alphabetical order.
The first one is done for you.

hungry get fish

F<u>ish get hungry</u>                                                    .

eat fish dolphins

D_____.

minnows little nap

L_____.

helps Dory Marlin

D_____.

whale speaks Dory

D_____.

**HINT** Look at the first letter of each word.

Write your own sentence using words in alphabetical order.

# Maze

Nemo and Peach want to find Gill. Follow the words in alphabetical order to find Gill!

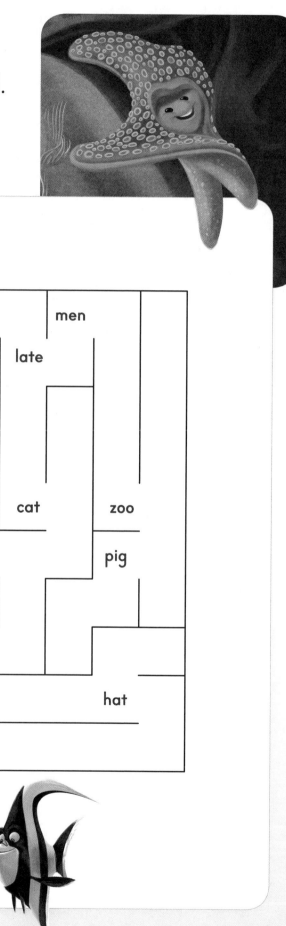

**Start**

bat

men

late

car

door

fish

eel

cat

zoo

pig

tell

got

hat

zoo

ice

**Finish**

# Matching

What does Nemo see? Say the word for the object in each picture. What sound do you hear at the beginning of the word? Match each picture to a letter sound.

b

h

f

# Matching

Ariel learns about different foods in Eric's world. (Circle) the words on each line that start with the same sound. The first one is done for you.

1. (tomato)   pepper   (turnip)   bean

2. pear   apple   orange   peach

3. carrot   beet   meat   kale

4. ham   jam   ginger   yam

5. lemon   wrap   taco   radish

6. ketchup   cake   mustard   pie

Write a sentence using two of the words that you circled.

_____

_____

**HINT** Two words on each line start with the same sound.

# Matching

The names of Ariel's sisters all end with an **a** sound, like Aquata and Arista! Say the word for each object. What sound do you hear at the end of the word? Match each picture to a letter sound.

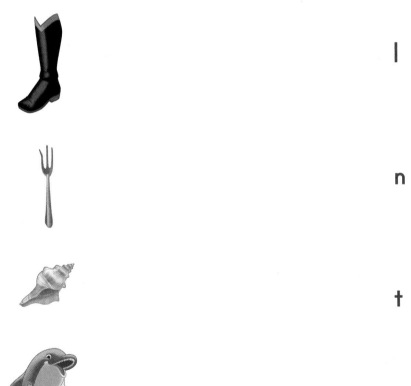

l

n

t

k

# Colour to Complete

What animal swallows Marlin and Dory? To find out, colour the picture. Use the Colour Key.

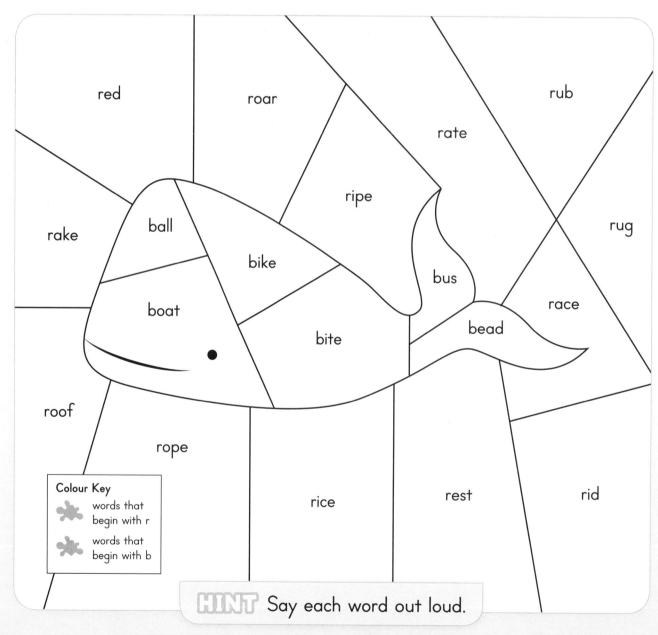

red

roar

rub

rate

ripe

rake

ball

bike

bus

rug

boat

bite

race

bead

roof

rope

**Colour Key**
words that begin with r
words that begin with b

rice

rest

rid

**HINT** Say each word out loud.

# Word Search

The word **jellyfish** starts with the letter j. Complete the word search. Find the words that start with the sound made by the letter j.

| | | | | | | | | | |
|---|---|---|---|---|---|---|---|---|---|
| R | J | E | W | E | L | R | X | | JAM |
| J | A | R | N | F | J | A | M | | JAR |
| K | Z | R | J | H | S | I | U | | JEWEL |
| J | O | I | N | L | J | Y | K | | JOIN |
| U | L | H | C | I | O | S | Y | | JOY |
| U | Z | P | D | M | Y | F | F | | JUMP |
| U | C | D | W | S | A | V | F | | |
| G | S | E | J | U | M | P | X | | |

**HINT** Look across each row for the letter j in each hidden word. Then check across and down for words in the list.

# Solve the Riddles

What is Flounder? The word rhymes with **wish** and starts with **f**. Flounder is a **fish**! Solve each riddle.

1. I start with the same sound as the **h** in **hand**. You can put me on your head.

   I am a ____ ____ ____.

2. I start with the same sound as the **p** in **pen**. You can swim in me.

   I am a ____ ____ ____ ____.

3. I start with the same sound as the **r** in **rat**. You can put me on your finger.

   I am a ____ ____ ____ ____.

4. I start with the same sound as the **c** in **cat**. You eat me at a birthday party.

   I am a ____ ____ ____ ____.

# Maze

Help Ariel find Flounder. Follow the words that start with the sound made by the letter **w**.

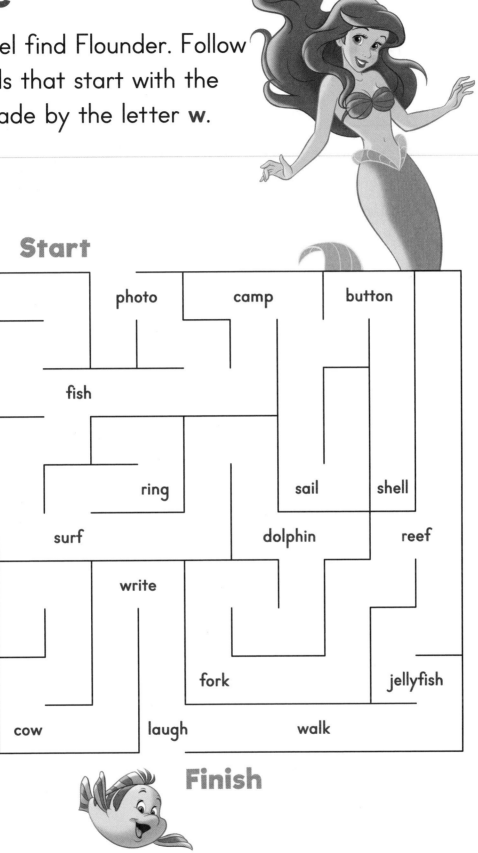

Start

photo     camp     button

fish

ring     sail     shell

surf     dolphin     reef

write

fork     jellyfish

cow     laugh     walk

Finish

# Fill In the Blanks

Ariel learns the words for a song. What will she sing about? Fill in each blank with the correct letter sound to find out. Then write a sentence with one of the words.

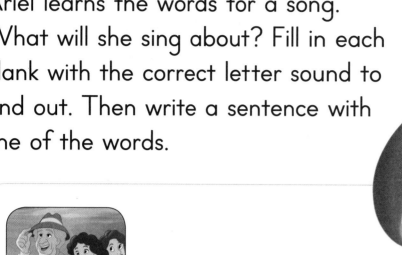

hu____ans

m

p

da____cing

r

n

wal____ing

k

x

_____

_____

**HINT** Look at the pictures for a clue to the word.

# Solve the Riddles

Ariel's sisters like to sing songs with rhymes. Solve each riddle by finding the rhyming word.

1. I am an animal. I say meow.

   I rhyme with **sat**.

   What am I? _____

2. I am something you wear.

   I keep you warm. I rhyme with **boat**.

   What am I? _____

3. I am yellow. I am high in the sky.

   I rhyme with **fun**.

   What am I? _____

4. I can go fast. You can drive me.

   I rhyme with **far**.

   What am I? _____

**HINT** Rhyming words sound the same.

# Fill In the Blanks

Complete each rhyming sentence. Fill in each missing rhyming word.

**Word Bank**

Way   fun   go   clue

Marlin is looking for his **son**.
He meets Dory who wants to have _____.

Marlin doesn't know what to **do**.
Then Dory finds a mask that has a _____.

The words are as clear as **day**.
It says "P. Sherman, 42 Wallaby _____."

Where's Nemo? Now they **know**.
It's time to swim. So off they_____!

**HINT** Rhyming words sound the same, but the endings aren't always spelled the same way.

# Colour to Complete

Mr. Ray is a great teacher. What words rhyme with **ray**? To find out, colour the picture. Use the Colour Key.

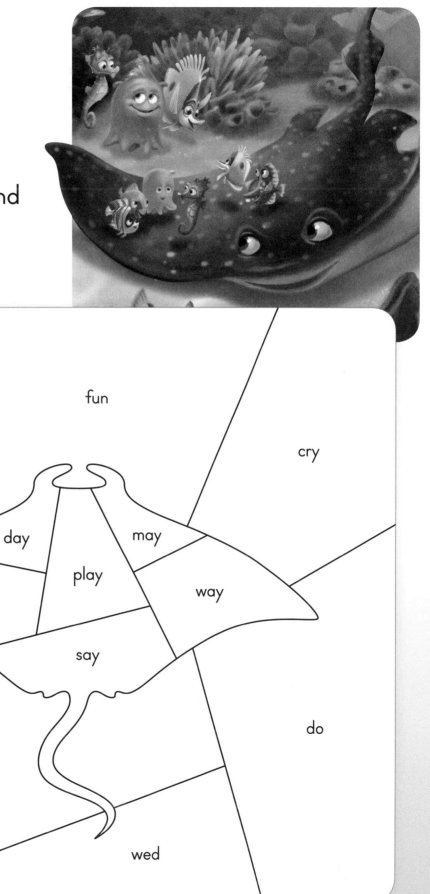

fun

fin

cry

day

may

play

tray

way

say

why

do

end

**Colour Key**

words that rhyme with ray

words that don't rhyme with ray

wed

# Fill In the Blanks

Fill in the blanks. Find out what Ariel and Flounder are doing.

**Word Bank**

do    is    are    get    be    go    can

Flounder and Ariel _____ having a race.

1, 2, 3 and off they _____!

Flounder _____ swim fast.

But Ariel _____ faster.

Who _____ you think will win? Ariel!

Will she _____ a prize?

What will it _____?

A piece of treasure!

**HINT** Try out the different sight words in each sentence. Which sight word makes sense?

# Unscramble the Words

Ariel and Flounder explore a ship.
Unscramble each sight word in **purple**.
Use the words to complete the story.

Ariel and Flounder _____ at the ship. **loko**

It is a _____ ship. **bgi**

What will _____ find inside? **tyeh**

Ariel hopes _____ will find treasures. **seh**

What do _____ think? **yuo**

Will she find something big or something

_____? **lttlei**

**HINT** The first letter of the scrambled word is in the correct spot.

# Word Search

Nemo and Sheldon might go here, there, or anywhere! Complete the word search. Find out where they go.

| | | | | | | | | |
|---|---|---|---|---|---|---|---|---|
| U | Q | W | J | N | P | K | L |
| N | O | V | E | R | E | N | S |
| D | K | A | T | H | E | R | E |
| E | H | F | R | O | C | N | R |
| R | A | W | A | Y | F | L | N |
| E | E | K | F | Y | W | B | M |
| X | P | Z | Z | O | U | T | M |
| L | C | E | D | O | W | N | I |

AWAY

DOWN

OUT

OVER

THERE

UNDER

**HINT** Look across each row for the first letter in each hidden word. Then check across and down for words in the list.

# Solve the Riddles

Fill in the sight words. Then solve each riddle.

**Word Bank**

of   am   very   two   a   in

1. I have a lot_____ teeth.

   They are _____ sharp.

   What am I? _____

2. I have _____ hard shell.

   I _____ green.

   What am I? _____

3. I fly _____ the air.

   I have _____ wings.

   What am I? _____

**HINT** Look at the pictures for clues.

# Fill In the Blanks

Where is Dory? To find out what Dory
is doing, fill in each blank.

### Word Bank

from    now    Where    for    will    play

_____ is Dory?

She hides _____ Squirt.

Squirt looks _____ Dory.

They like to _____ this game!

Who _____ hide next?

It's Squirt's turn _____!

# Maze

Nemo and his friends play hide-and-seek. Where is Sheldon? Follow the words that have a short vowel sound to find him.

**Start**

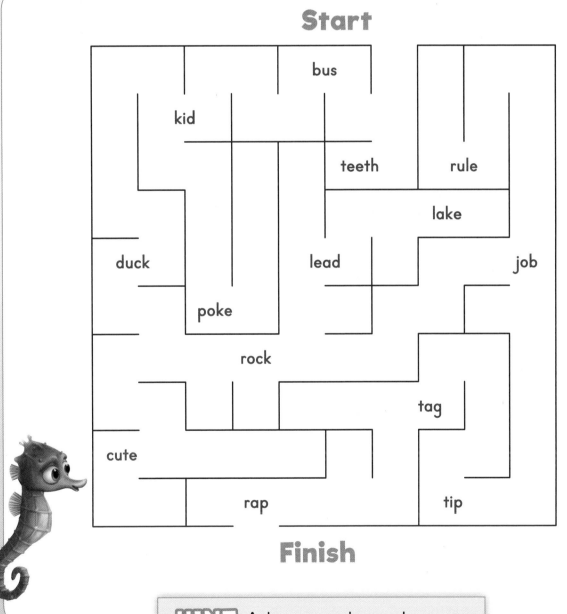

bus

kid

teeth     rule

lake

duck          lead          job

poke

rock

tag

cute

rap          tip

**Finish**

**HINT** A long vowel sound says its name. A short vowel sound doesn't.

37

# Fill In the Blanks

What foods are in Chef Louis's cupboard? To find out, fill in each word with the missing long vowel sound.

c\_\_\_ke

l\_\_\_me

m\_\_\_at

c\_\_\_ne

**HINT** A long vowel says its name.

# Colour to Complete

What does Sebastian like? To find out, colour the picture. Use the Colour Key.

kite

tube

need

bone

hose

late

pet

hug

dip

pack

dog

paint

mule

bean

**Colour Key**

long vowel sound

short vowel sound

# Fill In the Blanks

Ariel and Flounder **can** play **tag** for **fun**. Complete each word from the **-ag**, **-un**, and **-an** word families. Use the letters in the letter bank.

## Letter Bank

k   r   n   b   s   q   y   c   m   p

_____ag          _____un          _____an

_____ag          _____un          _____an

_____ag          _____un          _____an

_____ag          _____un          _____an

Write a sentence using one of the words from the **-ag**, **-un**, or **-an** word family.

_____

_____.

**HINT** Some letters will be used twice. Some letters will not be used at all.

# Maze

Ariel needs to find Prince Eric for a dance! To get to Eric, follow the words in the **-et** word family.

Start

| | |
|---|---|
| hat | bet |
| | get    let |
| pot | pet |
| wet | pen |
| | men |
| jet | bed    mad |
| | wig |
| met    set | tug |

Finish

# Solve the Riddles

Marlin gives Nemo something. It's soft and squishy. What is it? A **hug**! Solve the riddles using words from the **-ug** word family.

## Word Bank

hug    mug

lug    jug

bug    rug

1. I am very tiny. I am an insect. I have six legs.

   What am I? _____

2. I can have a pattern. You put me on the floor. I am made from cloth.

   What am I? _____

3. I am taller than a cup. You can fill me with juice. I have a handle too.

   What am I? _____

**HINT** Look at the words in the Word Bank that end with **-ug**.

# Fill In the Blanks

Marlin and Dory escape the whale! They **flop** on the dock. What are some other words in the **-op** word family?

_____op      _____op      _____op

_____op      _____op      _____op

_____op      _____op      _____op

Write a sentence using one of the words from the **-op** word family.

_____

_____

# Maze

Help Sebastian follow Ariel and Flounder. Find the words in the **-ig** and **-ip** word families to make it through the maze!

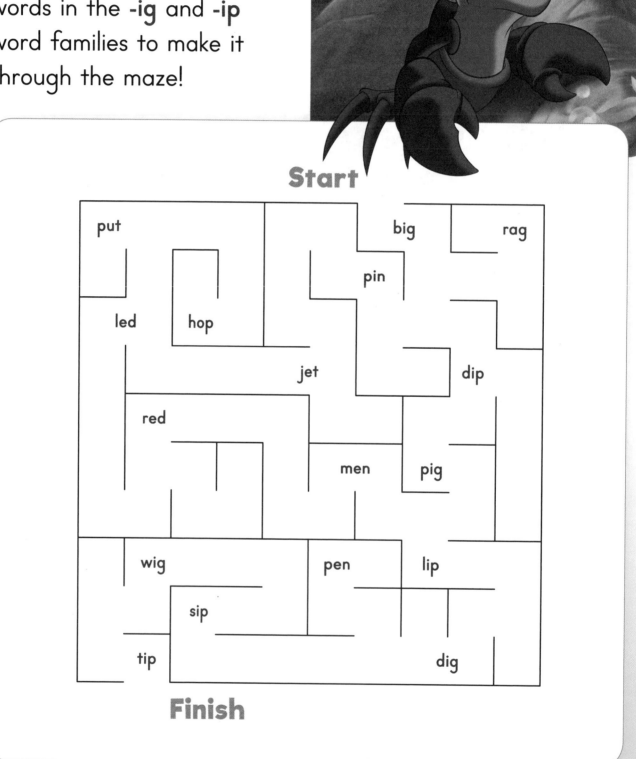

**Start**

put     big     rag

pin

led     hop

jet     dip

red

men     pig

wig     pen     lip

sip

tip     dig

**Finish**

# Colour to Complete

What does Ariel float on to get to Eric's ship? To find out, colour the picture. Use the Colour Key.

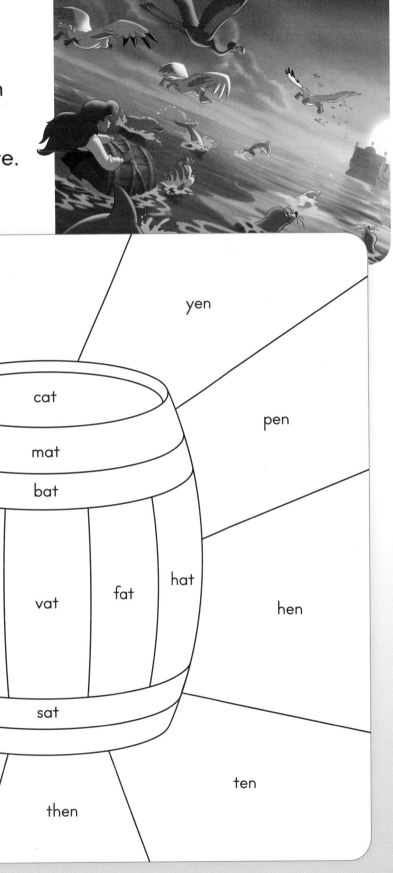

den

yen

cat

men

pen

mat

bat

rat

pat

vat

fat

hat

hen

zen

sat

**Colour Key**

words in the -en family

words in the -at family

when

then

ten

# Word Search

What colours does Nemo see in his world?
To find out, complete the word search.

| | | | | | | | | | |
|---|---|---|---|---|---|---|---|---|---|
| P | Z | N | E | C | J | P | E | | BLUE |
| G | R | E | E | N | K | I | N | | GREEN |
| E | W | D | B | N | Y | N | K | | PINK |
| X | W | Q | A | J | K | K | X | | PURPLE |
| F | Q | T | F | B | L | U | E | | RED |
| P | U | R | P | L | E | Z | K | | YELLOW |
| P | O | Y | E | L | L | O | W | | |
| J | R | E | D | J | M | O | S | | |

**HINT** Look across each row for the first letter in each hidden word. Then check across and down for words in the list.

# Maze

Nemo lives in the ocean, in a warm and sunny place. What kind of weather do you have? Follow the weather words to complete the maze.

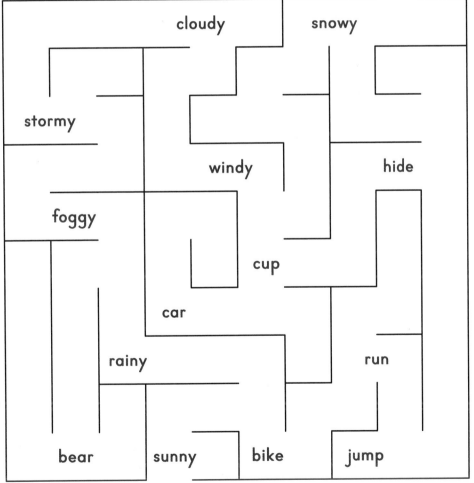

**Start**

cloudy    snowy

stormy

windy    hide

foggy

cup

car

rainy    run

bear    sunny    bike    jump

**Finish**

# Word Search

Ariel starts with the letter A!
So does the month of April!
Complete the word search to find
some of the months of the year.

| M | A | Y | O | G | N | H | A | | MARCH |
| M | A | R | C | H | Y | N | P | | APRIL |
| R | F | M | G | Z | X | V | R | | MAY |
| E | H | J | U | N | E | E | I | | JUNE |
| H | I | K | H | H | H | C | L | | JULY |
| A | J | F | H | J | U | L | Y | | AUGUST |
| A | U | G | U | S | T | R | K | | |
| W | N | N | S | C | Y | K | K | | |

**HINT** Look across each row for the first letter in each hidden word. Then look across and down to see if the whole word is there.

# Solve the Riddles

Eric is a prince. That is his job. What are some other jobs? Read the clues and fill in each blank.

**Word Bank**

letter    fire    police

1. I go up and down ladders.
   I ride in a big red truck.

   I'm a ___ ___ ___ ___ fighter.

2. I carry letters in a bag.
   I come whether it rains or snows.

   I'm a ___ ___ ___ ___ ___ ___ carrier.

3. If you get lost, you can ask me for help.
   I wear blue.

   I'm a ___ ___ ___ ___ ___ ___ officer.

# Colour to Complete

Nemo meets many friends in the tank. To find one of his friends, colour the picture. Use the Colour Key.

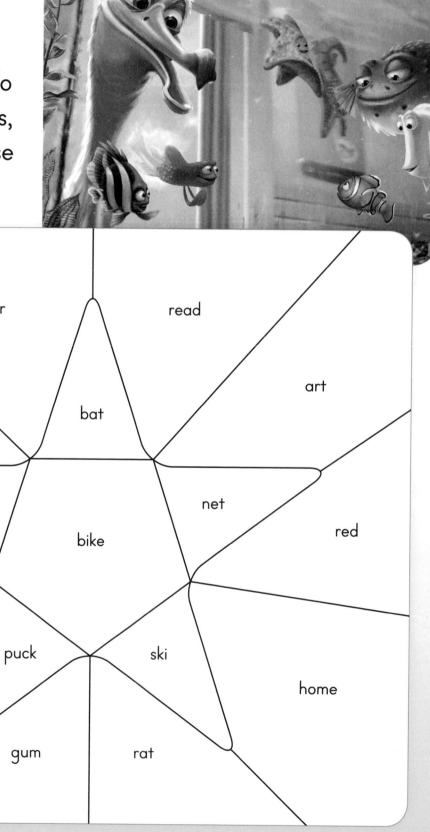

door

read

cat

bat

art

ball

net

bike

red

fog

pen

puck

ski

home

gum

rat

**Colour Key**

words about sports

other words

# Matching

Some fish are **big**. Some fish are **small**. Find more opposite pairs of words. Match the fish.

 small

 down

 cold

 slow

 fast

 big

 soft

 hot

 up

 hard

# Matching

Sir Grimsby is **old**. Eric is **young**. Old is the opposite of **young**. Match the opposite pairs of words.

tall                    out

in                      night

day                     full

happy                   sad

empty                   short

# Maze

Triton is **good** and Ursula is **bad**. **Good** is the opposite of **bad**. Find the opposite pairs to complete maze.

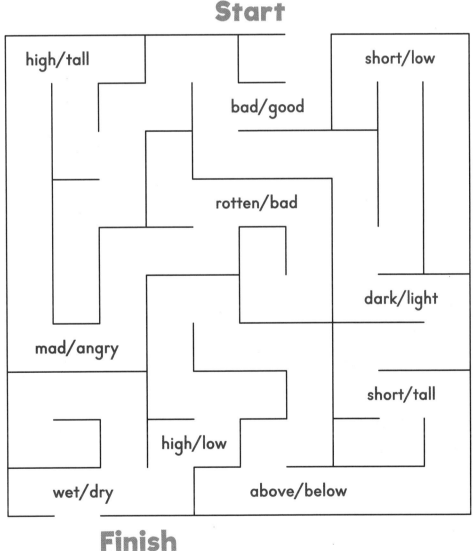

**Start**

high/tall    short/low

bad/good

rotten/bad

dark/light

mad/angry

short/tall

high/low

wet/dry    above/below

**Finish**

**HINT** Cross out the word pairs that are not opposites. Follow the other path.

# Solve the Rebus

There are many animals in the ocean. One animal is a **seahorse**. Seahorse is a compound word. Look at each picture. Write the compound word.

## Word Bank

ball     brush     bed     book

+ shelf = _____

hair + = _____

+ room = _____

eye + = _____

**HINT** Use the Word Bank to help you determine the word for each picture.

# Puzzle Pieces

Ariel looks for **seashells** under the sea. **Seashells** is a compound word. Match the puzzle pieces to create compound words. Then write a sentence with one of the compound words.

cat

sea

sail

sand

gull

boat

castle

fish

_____

_____

**HINT** Think of words that are made up of two smaller words.

# Maze

Dory is stung by a **jellyfish**! Follow the compound words to get to the end of the maze.

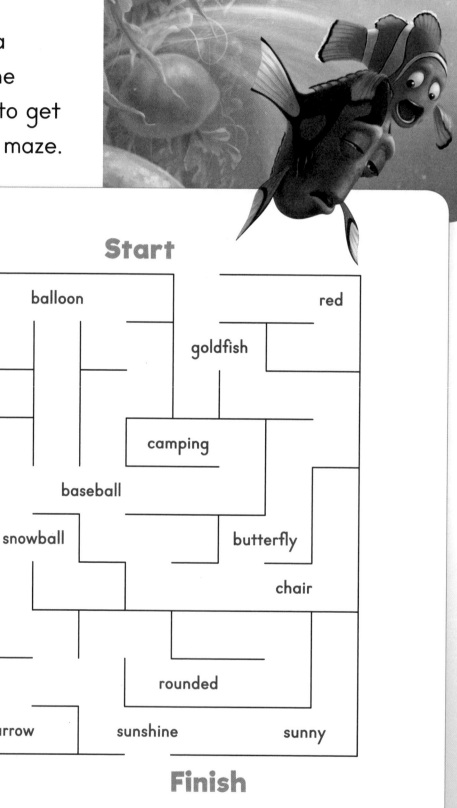

**Start**

balloon

red

goldfish

fishing

camping

baseball

class    snowball    butterfly

chair

rounded

narrow    sunshine    sunny

**Finish**

# Fill In the Blanks

Nemo **swims** in the sea. **Swim** is an action word.
Fill in the blanks with the best action word.

## Word Bank

laughs    jumps    look    cries

Nemo _____ at Bubbles.

Dory _____ because she
is upset.

Nemo and Peach _____
for their friends.

Nemo _____ in the air.

**HINT** Look at the pictures for a clue to the best action word.

# Unscramble the Words

Nemo is **happy**. How are Nemo's friends feeling? To find out, unscramble each word.

Marlin is **sda**. _____

Bubbles is **sdraec**. _____

Squirt is **hpypa**. _____

# Word Search

What words describe Nemo? To find out, complete the word search.

| | | | | | | | |
|---|---|---|---|---|---|---|---|
| E | O | Z | I | U | I | D | C |
| S | G | H | A | P | P | Y | L |
| S | M | A | L | L | Y | R | E |
| X | A | P | V | A | J | I | V |
| X | G | B | R | A | V | E | E |
| T | G | G | Z | I | X | M | R |
| O | F | U | N | R | U | X | P |
| E | S | M | A | R | T | X | V |

CLEVER

BRAVE

FUN

HAPPY

SMALL

SMART

**HINT** Look across each row for the first letter in each hidden word. Then check across and down for words in the list.

# Fill In the Blanks

Ariel can **see** the **sea**. The words **sea** and **see** are homophones. (Circle) the correct homophone. Then write the correct word.

what you say when you leave

buy/bye _____

what you did yesterday at dinnertime

ate/eight _____

two things that are matched together

pear/pair _____

Write a sentence using one of the homophones you didn't circle.

_____

**HINT** Homophones sound the same but have different meanings and spellings.

# Solve the Riddles

Prince Eric's ship needs a new **sail**.
Maybe Sir Grimsby can buy one on **sale**!
(Circle) the correct homophone to solve
each riddle.

1. I am used when you bake a cake.

   You scoop me up with a measuring cup.
   What am I?

   flower / flour

2. Many animals have me.
   I can be long or short.
   What am I?

   tale / tail

3. I am an animal that growls.
   I sleep during the winter.
   What am I?

   bear / bare

# Picture Search

The world around us is always changing!
Look at each picture. Circle the items in
picture 1 that are missing in picture 2.

1.

2.

How many items are missing from picture 1?

Count them and write the number. _____

# Fill In the Blanks

Fill in each blank. Complete the story.

**Word Bank**

voice   over   water   necklace
out   boat   bridge   potion

Eric takes Ariel for a ride. They

drive across the _____.

Eric and Ariel go on the

_____ in a _____.

Flotsam and Jetsam tip

the boat _____.

Ariel and Eric fall _____ of
the boat.

**HINT** Look at the pictures for clues.

Ursula creates a _____.

She wants to stop Ariel from seeing Eric.

Ursula pretends to be human.

She wears a _____ with Ariel's voice!

Finally, Ariel gets her _____ back!

# Picture Search

Look at the picture. Think
about the story it tells.
Answer each question.

What do you think the story will be about?

_____

_____

_____

What do you think will happen next?

_____

_____

_____

**HINT** When you make predictions, you figure out
what a story is about or what will happen next.

# Picture Search

Dory and Marlin are lost. They swim for a long time. Dory and Marlin meet a whale. Dory asks the whale to tell them the way.

Which picture shows what happens next?

_____

_____

How do you know?

_____

_____

# Out of Order

The pictures are out of order. Read the story. Then write a number in each box to put the pictures in order.

1. Nemo goes to school with Mr. Ray. Nemo makes lots of friends.

2. At the Drop-off, Nemo is taken by a diver! He is placed in a fish tank far from his father.

3. Nemo meets new friends in the fish tank. They come up with a plan for Nemo's escape!

4. Before he can escape, Nemo is put in a plastic bag. He is given to Darla. Nemo pretends he is not alive.

5. Darla shakes him! He jumps out of the bag! He goes down the drain to the ocean.

6. Finally, he sees his father, Marlin, again!

**HINT** Read the story and think about what happens first, second, and so on. Look at the pictures for clues.

# Solve the Rebus

Look at the picture of Ariel. Answer each rebus using the Word Bank. Then answer the question below.

**Word Bank**

belt    hat    sword    map

Ariel has a  _____.

Ariel has a  _____.

Ariel has a _____.

Ariel has a  _____.

What is Ariel dressed up as?

_____

**HINT** In a rebus puzzle, sometimes a word is replaced by a picture.

# Crack the Code

Read about Ariel and answer the questions. Use the letters in the squares to solve the mystery!

Ariel has red hair. Her friend Flounder is blue and yellow. Sebastian likes music. He is also Ariel's friend. Ariel meets Ursula. She is not nice.

1. What does Ariel have that is red?

2. Flounder is yellow and ___ ___ ___ ___ .

3. What does Sebastian like?

4. Sebastian is friends with whom?

5. Ursula is not ___ ___ ___ ___ .

What does Ariel become?

# Fill In the Blanks

Fill in each blank with the correct word.

Dory, Marlin, and Nemo live in the sea. The sea is made up of lots of water. The water in the sea is salty. Fish swim in the water. Plants also live in the sea. Some plants are green. Other plants are orange. Some fish eat plants.

The water in the sea is _____.

Fish swim in the _____.

_____ also live in the sea.

The plants are the colours _____ and

_____.

Some fish _____ plants.

# Solve the Rebus

Figure out what word each picture represents. Then answer the questions about Dory.

Dory is a  _____.

Dory can speak _____.

Dory likes to _____.

1. What is Dory?

_____

2. What can Dory speak?

_____

3. What does Dory like to do?

_____

Write your own sentence about Dory.

_____

# Picture Search

Read the text about each character. Look at each picture. Guess which character it is.

I am the King of the Sea. I wear a crown. I sit on a throne.

_____

I am a mermaid. I want to be human. I search for treasure.

_____

# Out of Order

Read the story about Ariel. Then
put the pictures in the right order.

Ariel is a mermaid. She lives in the sea. She misses an
important concert. She goes to the surface. King Triton
gets mad at her. Then she sees a ship. She visits the
ship to see what is going on. There's a big storm. Ariel
saves Prince Eric. King Triton finds out about Ariel's
treasures. He destroys them!

1

**HINT** The numeral 1 has been
placed in the correct picture for you.

# Out of Order

Nemo is a fish who is a long way from home. His father looks for him. Put the story in the right order. Match each picture to the paragraph that describes it.

1. Dory meets Marlin Marlin is sad because Nemo has been captured. Dory wants to help Marlin find Nemo.

2. Nemo is placed in a fish tank. He makes many new friends. Gill tells Nemo how to get out of the fish tank.

**HINT** The numeral 1 has been placed in the correct picture for you.

1

3. Marlin and Dory are looking for Nemo. They meet some sharks. The sharks want to be friends.

4. Nemo escapes from the fish tank. He gets trapped in a fishing net. Marlin and Dory find Nemo.

# Fill In the Blanks

During a big storm, Prince Eric falls overboard. Read the text about storms. Then fill in the blanks.

When the weather is stormy, the wind blows.

Often a lot of rain falls on the ground. The sky gets very dark.

Sometimes there is lightning. Lightning flashes in the sky.

When lightning flashes, there is also thunder.

Thunder is the loud sound that follows lightning.

Sometimes hail falls during a thunderstorm. Hail is rain that has frozen into ice.

During a big storm, you should stay inside to be safe.

During a storm, you can get wet when a lot of

_____ falls on the ground.

The sky gets very _____.

_____ flashes in the sky.

The loud sound that follows lightning is called

_____.

Rain that has frozen into ice is called _____.

During a big storm, you should stay _____
to be safe.

# Out of Order

Nemo has many friends. Read the words about Nemo's friends. Put the words in the right order.

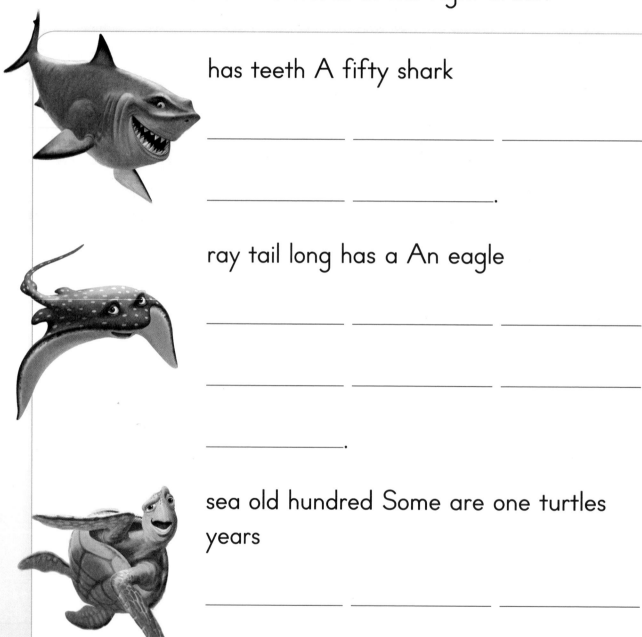

has teeth A fifty shark

_____ _____ _____

_____ _____ .

ray tail long has a An eagle

_____ _____ _____

_____ _____ _____

_____ .

sea old hundred Some are one turtles years

_____ _____ _____

_____ _____ _____

_____ _____ .

**HINT** The word with the capital letter goes first in the sentence.

# Solve the Rebus

Read the story about Nemo's friends. Can you figure out what the words are? Write the correct word in each space.

A C _____ turtle eats  _____.

They lay their _____ in a

_____ in the ground.

Their hard _____ protects them.

A sea _____ has gills, and fins.

Their body is covered with _____

that protect them.

An octopus has eight arms, three hearts,

and no _____.

# Fill In the Blanks

Ariel wants to be human. Read the story, then read the sentences about Ariel. Fill in the blanks so the sentences make sense. Use the Word Bank.

Ariel wants to live in the human world.

Ariel wants to walk.

Ariel wants to dance.

Ariel is sad.

Ariel's father sees that Ariel is sad.

He gives her two legs.

Ariel gets her wish.

Ariel becomes human.

Ariel will live in the human world.

Ariel is happy.

## Word Bank

happy   sad   walk   wish   human   dance

Ariel is _____ because she lives under the sea.

Ariel wants legs so she can _____ and

_____.

Ariel gets her _____.

Ariel becomes _____.

Ariel is _____ she will live in the human world.

# Colour to Complete

Gill is Nemo's friend. Colour the picture to see Gill. Use the Colour Key.

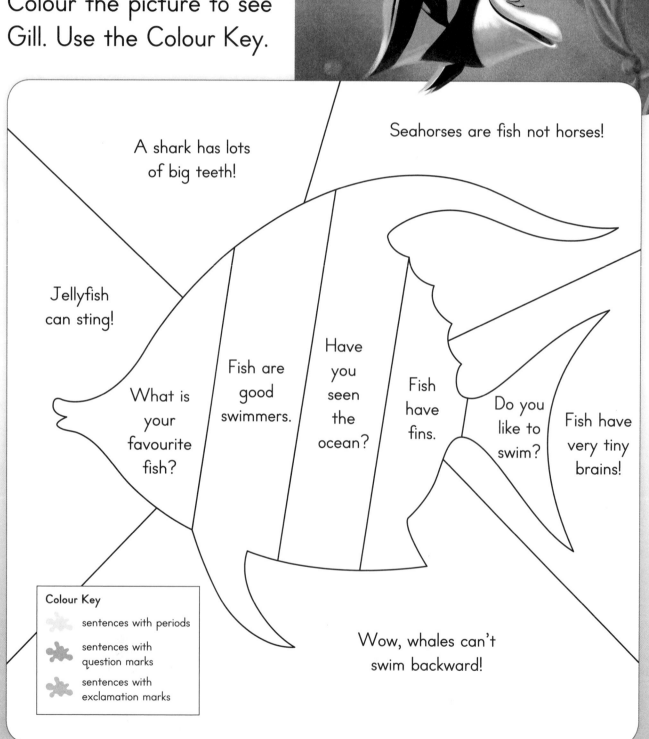

A shark has lots of big teeth!

Seahorses are fish not horses!

Jellyfish can sting!

What is your favourite fish?

Fish are good swimmers.

Have you seen the ocean?

Fish have fins.

Do you like to swim?

Fish have very tiny brains!

Wow, whales can't swim backward!

**Colour Key**

sentences with periods

sentences with question marks

sentences with exclamation marks

# Fill In the Blanks

What are Nemo and Crush doing? Complete each sentence with a period or an exclamation mark to find out.

### Punctuation

.    !

Nemo and Crush are having fun_____

They are swimming in the ocean_____

Here comes a big wave_____

They can ride the wave_____

Hooray_____

They did it_____

They can ride the next wave, too_____

Riding waves is so much fun_____

# Maze

Sebastian is late for the concert.
Find the correct path to help him
find the way. Look for the sentence
with the correct capitalization.

What music do you like

sebastian is late.

The concert is soon

Will Ariel be there?

# Fill In the Blanks

Ariel lives under the sea! Learn more about Ariel. Fill in the blanks with the missing pronouns.

**Word Bank**

they    you    He
Her    She    It

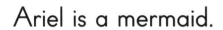

Ariel is a mermaid.

_____ loves adventure.

_____ friend is Flounder.

_____ is a guppy.

Together, _____ explore the ocean.

_____ is a lot of fun.

Do _____ like to go exploring?

**HINT** Some of the words start with capital letters.

# Solve the Riddles

Here are some riddles about Nemo's friends and the sea where they live. Can you solve them?

**Word Bank**

jellyfish    shell    sea star

1. I can be pink, orange, or other colours.
   I live in the ocean. I am a shape that you know.

   What am I? _____

2. I am round on top. I have long tentacles.
   I can sting you.

   What am I? _____

3. I am hard. I was someone's home.
   Some people like to collect me.

   What am I? _____

**HINT** The answer to each riddle is a person, place, or thing.

# Fill In the Blanks

Two of Nemo's friends are crabs. Learn more about them by filling in each blank.

## Word Bank

rocks   food   fish   legs   oceans

Crabs have two claws and eight _____.

Sometimes crabs hide under _____.

Crabs like to eat plants and _____.

The crabs hunt along the beach and ocean

floor for their _____.

Crabs live in all the world's _____.

# Maze

Ariel is looking for Sebastian. Get to the end of the maze by finding all the nouns!

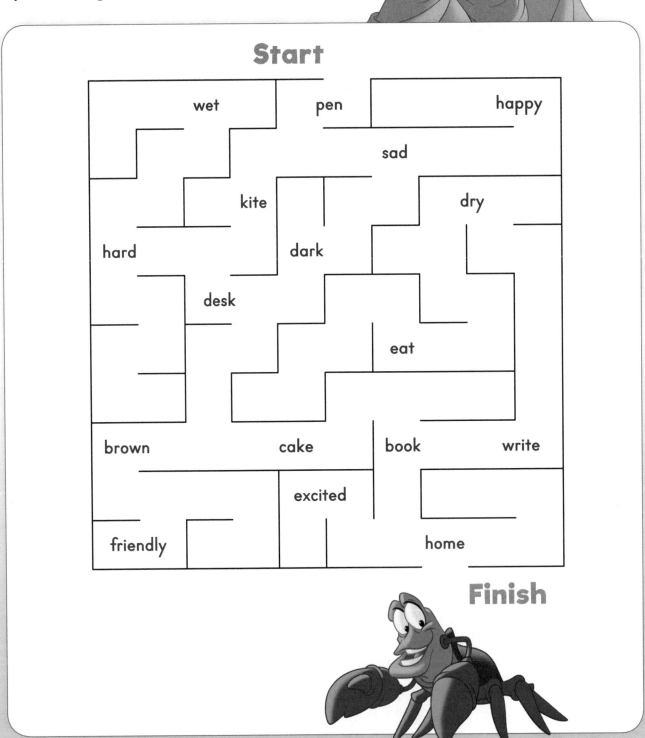

**Start**

wet    pen    happy

sad

kite    dry

hard    dark

desk

eat

brown    cake    book    write

excited

friendly    home

**Finish**

# Word Search

Ariel wants to be a part of the human world.
What does she want to do when she gets there?
Complete the word search to find out.

| | | | | | | | | |
|---|---|---|---|---|---|---|---|---|
| S | T | R | O | L | L | M | R | DANCE |
| J | T | W | R | U | N | K | T | JUMP |
| A | Y | P | S | T | J | K | J | RUN |
| D | A | N | C | E | B | S | N | STAND |
| A | T | R | C | X | T | L | W | STROLL |
| I | S | T | A | N | D | R | A | WALK |
| S | J | E | G | C | N | R | L | |
| J | U | M | P | J | D | D | K | |

# Solve the Riddles

Nemo and his friends can do many different things. Read the clues and write what each can do!

**Word Bank**

fly    swim    read

1. Nemo lives under water.
   Nemo uses fins to move.

   Nemo can _____!

2. Dory looks at words.
   Dory knows what they mean.

   Dory can _____!

3. Nigel flaps his wings.
   Nigel soars through the sky.

   Nigel can _____!

# Fill In the Blanks

There are lots of fun fish in the ocean. Learn more about them. Fill in the correct adjective.

**Word Bank**

yellow    hard    pointy    white

Mr. Ray has _____ spots.

Dory has a _____ tail.

Crush has a _____ shell.

Bruce has _____ teeth.

# Solve the Riddles

Ariel goes on many adventures in the ocean. Learn more about Ariel! (Circle) the correct adjective to solve the riddle!

1. When danger approaches, I go, go, go.

   I am a **slow/fast** swimmer.

2. When I am afraid, I face my fear.

   I am a **scared/brave** mermaid.

3. When I am with Prince Eric, I have fun.

   I am a **happy/sad** person.

4. After swimming all day, I yawn.

   I am a **tired/rested** mermaid.

5. When my sisters and I sing, everyone likes to listen.

   We are **amazing/terrible** singers.

# Fill In the Blanks

Ariel signs the contract Ursula gives her. A contract is a promise that is written down. Fill in each blank and make your own contract!

I promise to _____

_____.

I will also _____

_____.

I will not _____

_____.

Signed,

_____

your name

# Unscramble the Words

Read the story. Unscramble the words in the story so the story makes sense.

> ## Word Bank
>
> soon    him    happy    news    visit
>
> Nigel comes to **vtisi**. _____
>
> He has good **nwse**. _____
>
> Nigel tells Nemo his father is looking for **hmi**.
>
> _____
>
> Nemo is **hpapy**. _____
>
> Nemo hopes he will see his father **sono**.
>
> _____

# Solve the Riddle

Squirt and Nemo like to play a game. Read the poem about their game. Solve the riddle to find out what game they like to play.

Squirt wants to play!

What do you say?

We can swim fast.

Don't be last.

We swim round and round

But don't make a sound.

## Riddle

You need lots of room to play me.

You chase each other when you play me.

One of you is "it" when you play me.

What game am I? _____

# Picture Search

Look at the picture. Who is in the picture? What is happening? Write a sentence about this picture.

_____

_____

_____

_____

_____

# Fill In the Blanks

Imagine Ariel needs help to finish this letter to Sir Grimsby. Fill in the blanks with the missing words.

**Word Bank**

very   How   Eric   forward   tell

Dear Sir Grimsby,

_____ are you? I am _____ happy.

Prince _____ wants me to _____ you he misses you.

We hope you are very well. Eric and I look

_____ to seeing you again soon.

Your friend,
Ariel

# Answers

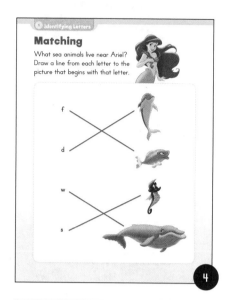

### Matching

What sea animals live near Ariel? Draw a line from each letter to the picture that begins with that letter.

f
d
w
s

**4**

### Solve the Riddles

Where does Ariel live? Solve the riddles. Then complete the mystery word to find out!

1. I am curved.
   The word **sun** starts with me.
   What letter am I? $\underset{1}{s}$

2. I am in the word **bee**.
   In fact, there are two of me.
   What letter am I? $\underset{2}{e}$

3. I am the first letter in the alphabet!
   The word **apple** starts with me.
   What letter am I? $\underset{3}{a}$

Mystery Word: $\underset{1}{s}\ \underset{2}{e}\ \underset{3}{a}$

**5**

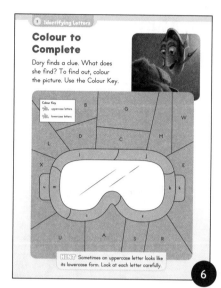

### Colour to Complete

Dory finds a clue. What does she find? To find out, colour the picture. Use the Colour Key.

Colour Key
🐟 uppercase letters
🐟 lowercase letters

**HINT** Sometimes an uppercase letter looks like its lowercase form. Look at each letter carefully.

**6**

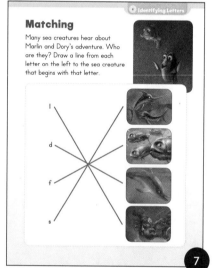

### Matching

Many sea creatures hear about Marlin and Dory's adventure. Who are they? Draw a line from each letter on the left to the sea creature that begins with that letter.

l
d
f
s

**7**

### Fill In the Blanks

Trace each missing letter. Read the story.

Ariel swims in the sea.

She swims with Flounder.

They see two whales.

The whales are happy.

Ariel and Flounder are happy too.

**8**

### Unscramble the Words

Ariel and Flounder find lots of treasure in the sea! Unscramble the letters to form words.

btoo
boot

frko
fork

jgu
jug

**HINT** The first letter in each word is in the correct spot.

**9**

### Puzzle Pieces

Nemo is exploring. What might he find? Trace the letter in each puzzle piece. Then write each word on the line.

b o a t

boat

l o g

log

**10**

### Fill In the Blanks

Trace each missing letter. Read the story.

Nemo is going to school.

Nemo likes school.

He sees his friends there.

He learns at school.

Nemo has lots of fun.

**11**

### Maze

Ariel needs to find her way to Eric's ship. Follow the lowercase letters through the maze.

Start

Finish

**HINT** Look carefully at each letter. Compare the size of letters.

**12**

*Sample answers provided.

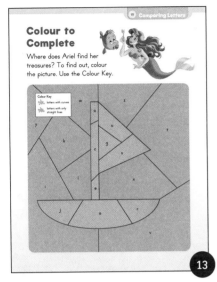

## Colour to Complete

Where does Ariel find her treasures? To find out, colour the picture. Use the Colour Key.

Colour Key
- letters with curves
- letters with only straight lines

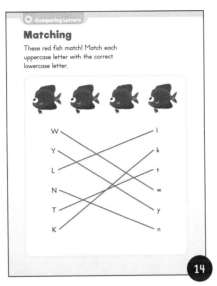

## Matching

These red fish match! Match each uppercase letter with the correct lowercase letter.

W — l
Y — k
L — t
N — w
T — y
K — n

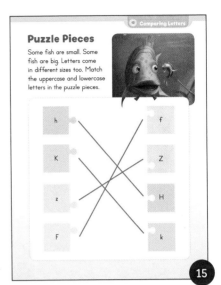

## Puzzle Pieces

Some fish are small. Some fish are big. Letters come in different sizes too. Match the uppercase and lowercase letters in the puzzle pieces.

h — f
K — Z
z — H
F — k

## Connect the Dots

Find out what Scuttle is holding. Connect the dots in alphabetical order.

HINT Start at a and then draw a line to b.

## Maze

Eric's dog, Max, is missing. Follow the letters in alphabetical order to lead Eric to Max.

Start

Finish

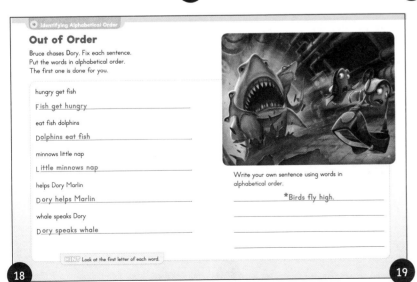

## Out of Order

Bruce chases Dory. Fix each sentence. Put the words in alphabetical order. The first one is done for you.

hungry get fish
Fish get hungry

eat fish dolphins
Dolphins eat fish

minnows little nap
Little minnows nap

helps Dory Marlin
Dory helps Marlin

whale speaks Dory
Dory speaks whale

HINT Look at the first letter of each word.

Write your own sentence using words in alphabetical order.

*Birds fly high.

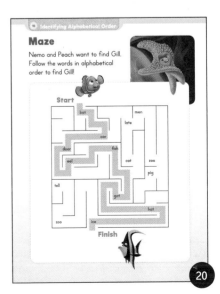

## Maze

Nemo and Peach want to find Gill. Follow the words in alphabetical order to find Gill!

Start

bat — men
late
car
door — fish
eel — cat — zoo
pig
tell
got
hat
zoo — ice

Finish

*Sample answers provided.

# Answers

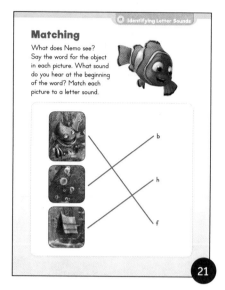

## Matching

What does Nemo see? Say the word for the object in each picture. What sound do you hear at the beginning of the word? Match each picture to a letter sound.

b
h
f

**21**

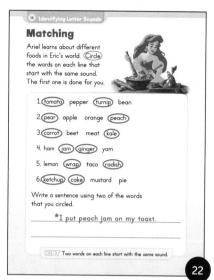

## Matching

Ariel learns about different foods in Eric's world. Circle the words on each line that start with the same sound. The first one is done for you.

1. (tomato) pepper (turnip) bean
2. (pear) apple orange (peach)
3. (carrot) beet meat (kale)
4. ham (jam) (ginger) yam
5. lemon (wrap) taco (radish)
6. (ketchup) (cake) mustard pie

Write a sentence using two of the words that you circled.

*I put peach jam on my toast.

**HINT** Two words on each line start with the same sound.

**22**

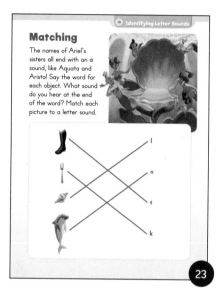

## Matching

The names of Ariel's sisters all end with an n sound, like Aquata and Arista! Say the word for each object. What sound do you hear at the end of the word? Match each picture to a letter sound.

l
n
t
k

**23**

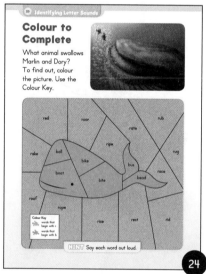

## Colour to Complete

What animal swallows Marlin and Dory? To find out, colour the picture. Use the Colour Key.

red roar rub
rate
rake ball ripe
bike rug
boat bus
bite bead race
roof
rope
rice rest rid

Colour Key
words that begin with r
words that begin with b

**HINT** Say each word out loud.

**24**

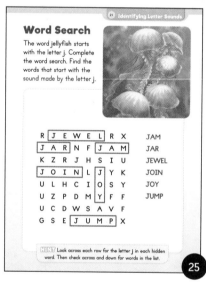

## Word Search

The word jellyfish starts with the letter j. Complete the word search. Find the words that start with the sound made by the letter j.

| R | J | E | W | E | L | R | X |
|---|---|---|---|---|---|---|---|
| J | A | R | N | F | J | A | M |
| K | Z | R | J | H | S | I | U |
| J | O | I | N | L | J | Y | K |
| U | L | H | C | I | O | S | Y |
| U | Z | P | D | M | Y | F | F |
| U | C | D | W | S | A | V | F |
| G | S | E | J | U | M | P | X |

JAM
JAR
JEWEL
JOIN
JOY
JUMP

**HINT** Look across each row for the letter j in each hidden word. Then check across and down for words in the list.

**25**

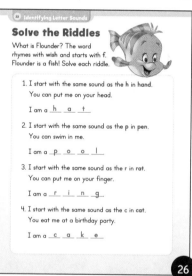

## Solve the Riddles

What is Flounder? The word rhymes with wish and starts with f. Flounder is a fish! Solve each riddle.

1. I start with the same sound as the h in hand. You can put me on your head.

   I am a _h_ _a_ _t_

2. I start with the same sound as the p in pen. You can swim in me.

   I am a _p_ _o_ _o_ _l_

3. I start with the same sound as the r in rat. You can put me on your finger.

   I am a _r_ _i_ _n_ _g_

4. I start with the same sound as the c in cat. You eat me at a birthday party.

   I am a _c_ _a_ _k_ _e_

**26**

## Maze

Help Ariel find Flounder. Follow the words that start with the sound made by the letter w.

Start

photo camp button
fish
ring sail shell
surf dolphin reef
write
fork jellyfish
cow laugh walk

Finish

**27**

## Fill In the Blanks

Ariel learns the words for a song. What will she sing about? Fill in each blank with the correct letter sound to find out. Then write a sentence with one of the words.

hu_m_ans
m
P

da_n_cing
r
n

wal_k_ing
k
x

*Dancing is fun.

**HINT** Look at the pictures for a clue to the word.

**28**

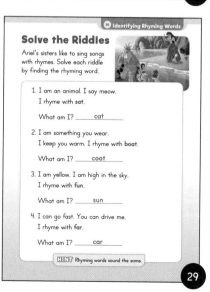

## Solve the Riddles

Ariel's sisters like to sing songs with rhymes. Solve each riddle by finding the rhyming word.

1. I am an animal. I say meow. I rhyme with sat.

   What am I? _cat_

2. I am something you wear. I keep you warm. I rhyme with boat.

   What am I? _coat_

3. I am yellow. I am high in the sky. I rhyme with fun.

   What am I? _sun_

4. I can go fast. You can drive me. I rhyme with far.

   What am I? _car_

**HINT** Rhyming words sound the same.

**29**

**102**

*Sample answers provided.

## Fill In the Blanks

Complete each rhyming sentence. Fill in each missing rhyming word.

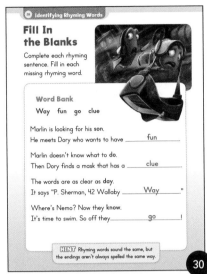

**Word Bank**

Way fun go clue

Marlin is looking for his **son**.
He meets Dory who wants to have _____ fun

Marlin doesn't know what to **do**.
Then Dory finds a mask that has a _____ clue

The words are as clear as **day**.
It says "P. Sherman, 42 Wallaby _____ Way "

Where's Nemo? Now they **know**.
It's time to swim. So off they _____ go !

**HINT** Rhyming words sound the same, but the endings aren't always spelled the same way.

**30**

---

## Colour to Complete

Mr. Ray is a great teacher. What words rhyme with ray? To find out, colour the picture. Use the Colour Key.

Colour Key
words that rhyme with ray
words that don't rhyme with ray

**31**

---

## Fill In the Blanks

Fill in the blanks. Find out what Ariel and Flounder are doing.

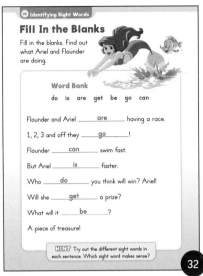

**Word Bank**

do is are get be go can

Flounder and Ariel _____ are having a race.

1, 2, 3 and off they _____ go !

Flounder _____ can swim fast.

But Ariel _____ is faster.

Who _____ do you think will win? Ariel!

Will she _____ get a prize?

What will it _____ be ?

A piece of treasure!

**HINT** Try out the different sight words in each sentence. Which sight word makes sense?

**32**

---

## Unscramble the Words

Ariel and Flounder explore a ship. Unscramble each sight word in **purple**. Use the words to complete the story.

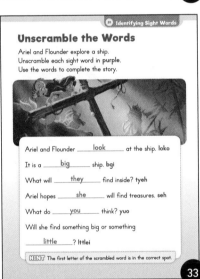

Ariel and Flounder _____ look at the ship. loko

It is a _____ big ship. bgi

What will _____ they find inside? tyeh

Ariel hopes _____ she will find treasures. seh

What do _____ you think? yuo

Will she find something big or something

_____ little ? lttlei

**HINT** The first letter of the scrambled word is in the correct spot.

**33**

---

## Word Search

Nemo and Sheldon might go here, there, or anywhere! Complete the word search. Find out where they go.

| U | Q | W | J | N | P | K | L |
|---|---|---|---|---|---|---|---|
| N | O | V | E | R | E | N | S |
| D | K | A | T | H | E | R | E |
| E | H | F | R | O | C | N | R |
| R | A | W | A | Y | F | L | N |
| E | E | K | F | Y | W | B | M |
| X | P | Z | Z | O | U | T | M |
| L | C | E | D | O | W | N | I |

AWAY
DOWN
OUT
OVER
THERE
UNDER

**HINT** Look across each row for the first letter in each hidden word. Then check across and down for words in the list.

**34**

---

## Solve the Riddles

Fill in the sight words. Then solve each riddle.

**Word Bank**

of am very two a in

1. I have a lot _____ of teeth.
   They are _____ very sharp.
   What am I? _____ shark

2. I have _____ a hard shell.
   I _____ am green.
   What am I? _____ sea turtle

3. I fly _____ in the air.
   I have _____ two wings.
   What am I? _____ bird

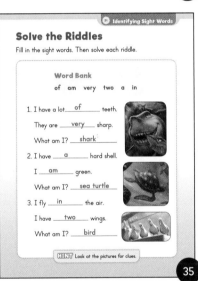

**HINT** Look at the pictures for clues.

**35**

---

## Fill In the Blanks

Where is Dory? To find out what Dory is doing, fill in each blank.

**Word Bank**

from now Where for will play

_____ Where is Dory?

She hides _____ from Squirt.

Squirt looks _____ for Dory.

They like to _____ play this game!

Who _____ will hide next?

It's Squirt's turn _____ now !

**36**

---

## Maze

Nemo and his friends play hide-and-seek. Where is Sheldon? Follow the words that have a short vowel sound to find him.

Start

bus
kid
teeth
rule
duck
lake
lead
job
poke
rock
tag
cute
rap
tip
Finish

**HINT** A long vowel sound says its name. A short vowel sound doesn't.

**37**

---

## Fill In the Blanks

What foods are in Chef Louis's cupboard? To find out, fill in each word with the missing long vowel sound.

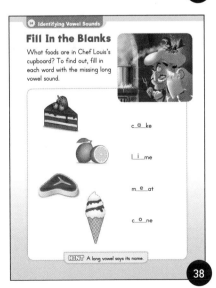

c a ke

l i me

m e at

c o ne

**HINT** A long vowel says its name.

**38**

---

\*Sample answers provided.

# Answers

### Colour to Complete
*Identifying Vowel Sounds*

What does Sebastian like? To find out, colour the picture. Use the Colour Key.

**39**

### Fill In the Blanks
*Forming Words*

Ariel and Flounder can play tag for fun. Complete each word from the -ag, -un, and -an word families. Use the letters in the letter bank.

**Letter Bank**

k r n b s q y c m p

| | | |
|---|---|---|
| r_ag | r_un | r_an |
| n_ag | n_un | c_an |
| b_ag | b_un | m_an |
| s_ag | s_un | p_an |

Write a sentence using one of the words from the -ag, -un, or -an word family.

*I carry a blue bag to school.

**HINT** Some letters will be used twice. Some letters will not be used at all.

**40**

### Maze
*Forming Words*

Ariel needs to find Prince Eric for a dance! To get to Eric, follow the words in the -et word family.

**41**

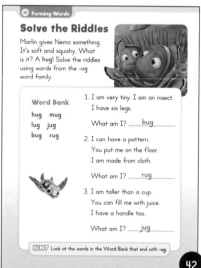

### Solve the Riddles
*Forming Words*

Marlin gives Nemo something. It's soft and squishy. What is it? A hug! Solve the riddles using words from the -ug word family.

**Word Bank**

hug mug
lug jug
bug rug

1. I am very tiny. I am an insect. I have six legs.

   What am I? bug

2. I can have a pattern. You put me on the floor. I am made from cloth.

   What am I? rug

3. I am taller than a cup. You can fill me with juice. I have a handle too.

   What am I? jug

**HINT** Look at the words in the Word Bank that end with -ug.

**42**

### Fill In the Blanks
*Forming Words*

Marlin and Dory escape the whale! They flop on the dock. What are some other words in the -op word family?

| | | |
|---|---|---|
| c_op | p_op | pl_op |
| h_op | t_op | dr_op |
| m_op | cr_op | st_op |

Write a sentence using one of the words from the -op word family.

*A bunny can hop.

**43**

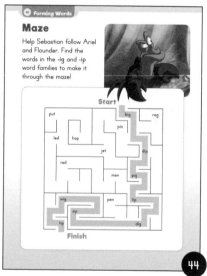

### Maze
*Forming Words*

Help Sebastian follow Ariel and Flounder. Find the words in the -ig and -ip word families to make it through the maze!

**44**

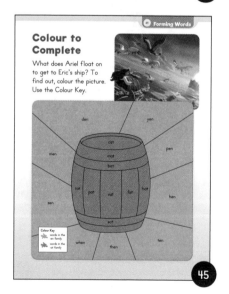

### Colour to Complete
*Forming Words*

What does Ariel float on to get to Eric's ship? To find out, colour the picture. Use the Colour Key.

**45**

### Word Search
*Understanding Vocabulary*

What colours does Nemo see in his world? To find out, complete the word search.

| P | Z | N | E | C | J | P | E | | BLUE |
|---|---|---|---|---|---|---|---|---|---|
| G | R | E | E | N | K | I | N | | GREEN |
| E | W | D | B | N | Y | N | K | | PINK |
| X | W | Q | A | J | K | K | X | | PURPLE |
| F | Q | T | F | B | L | U | E | | RED |
| P | U | R | P | L | E | Z | K | | YELLOW |
| P | O | Y | E | L | L | O | W | | |
| J | R | E | D | J | M | O | S | | |

**HINT** Look across each row for the first letter in each hidden word. Then check across and down for words in the list.

**46**

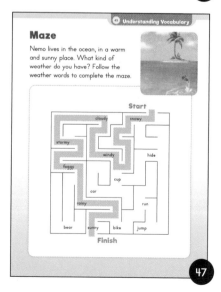

### Maze
*Understanding Vocabulary*

Nemo lives in the ocean, in a warm and sunny place. What kind of weather do you have? Follow the weather words to complete the maze.

**47**

**104**

*Sample answers provided.

## Word Search

Ariel starts with the letter A! So does the month of April! Complete the word search to find some of the months of the year.

| M | A | Y | O | G | N | H | A |
|---|---|---|---|---|---|---|---|
| M | A | R | C | H | Y | N | P |
| R | F | M | G | Z | X | V | R |
| E | H | J | U | N | E | E | I |
| H | I | K | H | H | H | C | L |
| A | J | F | H | J | U | L | Y |
| A | U | G | U | S | T | R | K |
| W | N | N | S | C | Y | K | K |

MARCH
APRIL
MAY
JUNE
JULY
AUGUST

**HINT** Look across each row for the first letter in each hidden word. Then look across and down to see if the whole word is there.

48

---

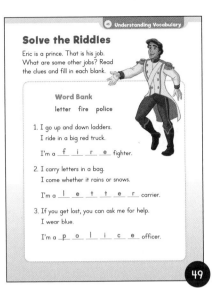

## Solve the Riddles

Eric is a prince. That is his job. What are some other jobs? Read the clues and fill in each blank.

**Word Bank**
letter   fire   police

1. I go up and down ladders.
   I ride in a big red truck.

   I'm a f i r e fighter.

2. I carry letters in a bag.
   I come whether it rains or snows.

   I'm a l e t t e r carrier.

3. If you get lost, you can ask me for help.
   I wear blue.

   I'm a p o l i c e officer.

49

---

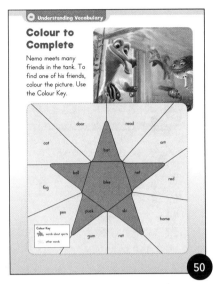

## Colour to Complete

Nemo meets many friends in the tank. To find one of his friends, colour the picture. Use the Colour Key.

door   read
cat   art
bat
ball   net   red
fog   bike
pen   puck   ski
home
gum   rat

**Colour Key**
words about sports
other words

50

---

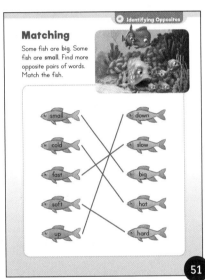

## Matching

Some fish are **big**. Some fish are **small**. Find more opposite pairs of words. Match the fish.

small — hard
cold — slow
fast — big
soft — hot
up — down

51

---

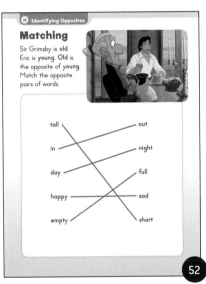

## Matching

Sir Grimsby is **old**. Eric is **young**. **Old** is the opposite of **young**. Match the opposite pairs of words.

tall — out
in — night
day — full
happy — sad
empty — short

52

---

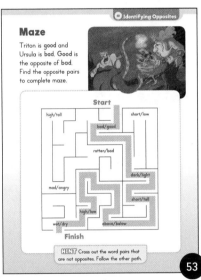

## Maze

Triton is **good** and Ursula is **bad**. **Good** is the opposite of **bad**. Find the opposite pairs to complete maze.

**Start**

high/tall   short/low
bad/good
rotten/bad
dark/light
mad/angry
short/tall
high/low
wet/dry   above/below

**Finish**

**HINT** Cross out the word pairs that are not opposites. Follow the other path.

53

---

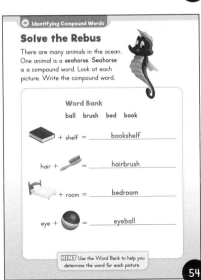

## Solve the Rebus

There are many animals in the ocean. One animal is a **seahorse**. Seahorse is a compound word. Look at each picture. Write the compound word.

**Word Bank**
ball   brush   bed   book

+ shelf = bookshelf

hair + = hairbrush

+ room = bedroom

eye + = eyeball

**HINT** Use the Word Bank to help you determine the word for each picture.

54

---

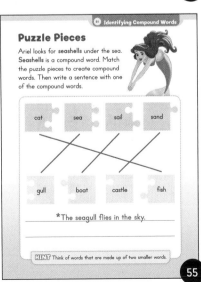

## Puzzle Pieces

Ariel looks for **seashells** under the sea. Seashells is a compound word. Match the puzzle pieces to create compound words. Then write a sentence with one of the compound words.

cat   sea   sail   sand

gull   boat   castle   fish

*The seagull flies in the sky.

**HINT** Think of words that are made up of two smaller words.

55

---

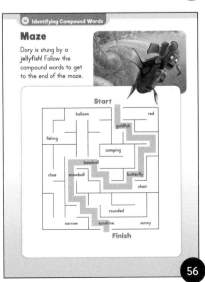

## Maze

Dory is stung by a **jellyfish**! Follow the compound words to get to the end of the maze.

**Start**

balloon   red
goldfish
fishing
camping
baseball
class   snowball   butterfly
chair
rounded
narrow   sunshine   sunny

**Finish**

56

---

*Sample answers provided.

**105**

# Answers

## Fill In the Blanks

Nemo swims in the sea. Swim is an action word.
Fill in the blanks with the best action word.

**Word Bank**

laughs  jumps  look  cries

Nemo ___laughs___ at Bubbles.

Dory ___cries___ because she is upset.

Nemo and Peach ___look___ for their friends.

Nemo ___jumps___ in the air.

HINT Look at the pictures for a clue to the best action word.

**57**

## Unscramble the Words

Nemo is happy. How are Nemo's friends feeling? To find out, unscramble each word.

Marlin is sda. ___sad___

Bubbles is sdraec. ___scared___

Squirt is hpypa. ___happy___

**58**

## Word Search

What words describe Nemo? To find out, complete the word search.

| E | O | Z | I | U | I | D | C |
|---|---|---|---|---|---|---|---|
| S | G | H | A | P | P | Y | L |
| S | M | A | L | L | Y | R | E |
| X | A | P | V | A | J | I | V |
| X | G | B | R | A | V | E | E |
| T | G | G | Z | I | X | M | R |
| O | F | U | N | R | U | X | P |
| E | S | M | A | R | T | X | V |

CLEVER
BRAVE
FUN
HAPPY
SMALL
SMART

HINT Look across each row for the first letter in each hidden word. Then check across and down for words in the list.

**59**

## Fill In the Blanks

Ariel can see the sea. The words sea and see are homophones. Circle the correct homophone. Then write the correct word.

what you say when you leave

buy / (bye) ___bye___

what you did yesterday at dinnertime

(ate) / eight ___ate___

two things that are matched together

pear / (pair) ___pair___

Write a sentence using one of the homophones you didn't circle.

___*I love eating pears.___

HINT Homophones sound the same but have different meanings and spellings.

**60**

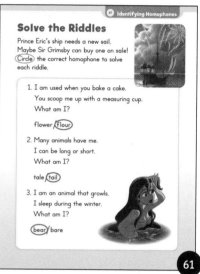

## Solve the Riddles

Prince Eric's ship needs a new sail. Maybe Sir Grimsby can buy one on sale! Circle the correct homophone to solve each riddle.

1. I am used when you bake a cake. You scoop me up with a measuring cup. What am I?

   flower / (flour)

2. Many animals have me. I can be long or short. What am I?

   tale / (tail)

3. I am an animal that growls. I sleep during the winter. What am I?

   (bear) / bare

**61**

## Picture Search

The world around us is always changing! Look at each picture. Circle the items in picture 1 that are missing in picture 2.

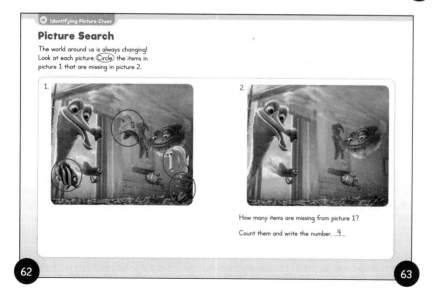

1.

2.

How many items are missing from picture 1?
Count them and write the number. ___4___

**62**    **63**

**106**

*Sample answers provided.

## Fill In the Blanks

Fill in each blank. Complete the story.

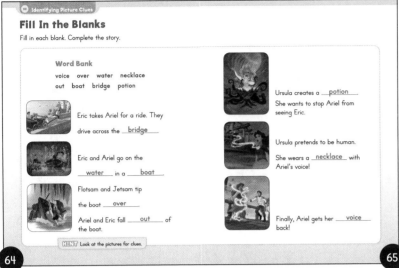

**Word Bank**

voice  over  water  necklace
out  boat  bridge  potion

Eric takes Ariel for a ride. They drive across the __bridge__.

Eric and Ariel go on the __water__ in a __boat__.

Flotsam and Jetsam tip the boat __over__.

Ariel and Eric fall __out__ of the boat.

Ursula creates a __potion__. She wants to stop Ariel from seeing Eric.

Ursula pretends to be human. She wears a __necklace__ with Ariel's voice!

Finally, Ariel gets her __voice__ back!

**HINT** Look at the pictures for clues.

64  65

## Picture Search

Look at the picture. Think about the story it tells. Answer each question.

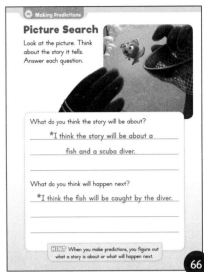

What do you think the story will be about?

__*I think the story will be about a fish and a scuba diver.__

What do you think will happen next?

__*I think the fish will be caught by the diver.__

**HINT** When you make predictions, you figure out what a story is about or what will happen next.

66

## Picture Search

Dory and Marlin are lost. They swim for a long time. Dory and Marlin meet a whale. Dory asks the whale to tell them the way.

Which picture shows what happens next?

__*The first picture shows what happens next.__

How do you know?

__*It shows Dory, Marlin and a whale's throat. The other picture shows fish that aren't in the story.__

67

## Out of Order

The pictures are out of order. Read the story. Then write a number in each box to put the pictures in order.

1. Nemo goes to school with Mr. Ray. Nemo makes lots of friends.

2. At the Drop-off, Nemo is taken by a diver! He is placed in a fish tank far from his father.

3. Nemo meets new friends in the fish tank. They come up with a plan for Nemo's escape!

4. Before he can escape, Nemo is put in a plastic bag. He is given to Darla. Nemo pretends he is not alive.

5. Darla shakes him! He jumps out of the bag! He goes down the drain to the ocean.

6. Finally, he sees his father, Marlin, again!

**HINT** Read the story and think about what happens first, second, and so on. Look at the pictures for clues.

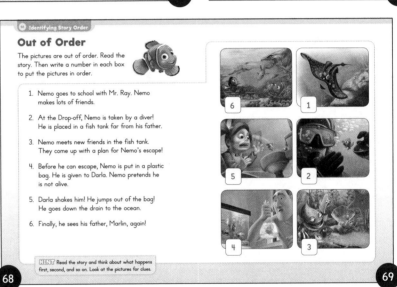

68  69

## Solve the Rebus

Look at the picture of Ariel. Answer each rebus using the Word Bank. Then answer the question below.

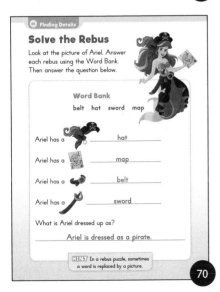

**Word Bank**

belt  hat  sword  map

Ariel has a __hat__.

Ariel has a __map__.

Ariel has a __belt__.

Ariel has a __sword__.

What is Ariel dressed up as?

__Ariel is dressed as a pirate.__

**HINT** In a rebus puzzle, sometimes a word is replaced by a picture.

70

## Crack the Code

Read about Ariel and answer the questions. Use the letters in the squares to solve the mystery!

Ariel has red hair. Her friend Flounder is blue and yellow. Sebastian likes music. He is also Ariel's friend. Ariel meets Ursula. She is not nice.

1. What does Ariel have that is red?

   h a i r

2. Flounder is yellow and b l u e

3. What does Sebastian like?

   m u s i c

4. Sebastian is friends with whom?

   A r i e l

5. Ursula is not n i c e

What does Ariel become?

h u m a n

71

## Fill In the Blanks

Fill in each blank with the correct word.

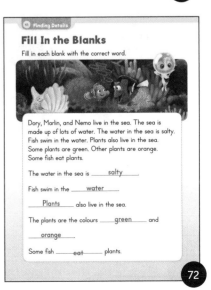

Dory, Marlin, and Nemo live in the sea. The sea is made up of lots of water. The water in the sea is salty. Fish swim in the water. Plants also live in the sea. Some plants are green. Other plants are orange. Some fish eat plants.

The water in the sea is __salty__.

Fish swim in the __water__.

__Plants__ also live in the sea.

The plants are the colours __green__ and __orange__.

Some fish __eat__ plants.

72

*Sample answers provided.

**107**

# Answers

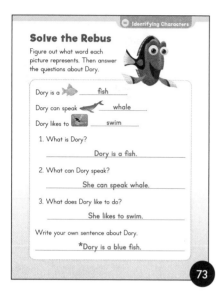

## Solve the Rebus

Figure out what word each picture represents. Then answer the questions about Dory.

Dory is a 🐟 **fish**

Dory can speak 🐋 **whale**

Dory likes to 🐟 **swim**

1. What is Dory?

   **Dory is a fish.**

2. What can Dory speak?

   **She can speak whale.**

3. What does Dory like to do?

   **She likes to swim.**

Write your own sentence about Dory.

   ***Dory is a blue fish.**

**73**

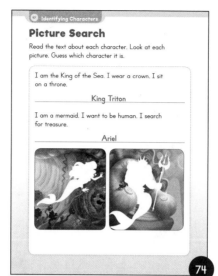

## Picture Search

Read the text about each character. Look at each picture. Guess which character it is.

I am the King of the Sea. I wear a crown. I sit on a throne.

**King Triton**

I am a mermaid. I want to be human. I search for treasure.

**Ariel**

**74**

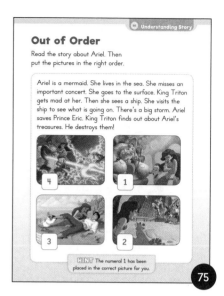

## Out of Order

Read the story about Ariel. Then put the pictures in the right order.

Ariel is a mermaid. She lives in the sea. She misses an important concert. She goes to the surface. King Triton gets mad at her. Then she sees a ship. She visits the ship to see what is going on. There's a big storm. Ariel saves Prince Eric. King Triton finds out about Ariel's treasures. He destroys them!

4 | 1
3 | 2

**HINT** The numeral 1 has been placed in the correct picture for you.

**75**

## Out of Order

Nemo is a fish who is a long way from home. His father looks for him. Put the story in the right order. Match each picture to the paragraph that describes it.

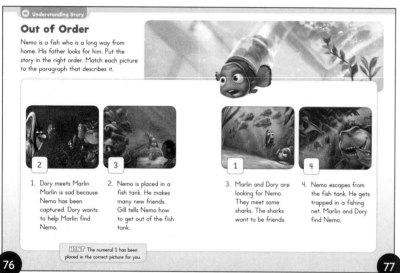

2 | 3 | 1 | 4

1. Dory meets Marlin. Marlin is sad because Nemo has been captured. Dory wants to help Marlin find Nemo.

2. Nemo is placed in a fish tank. He makes many new friends. Gill tells Nemo how to get out of the fish tank.

3. Marlin and Dory are looking for Nemo. They meet some sharks. The sharks want to be friends.

4. Nemo escapes from the fish tank. He gets trapped in a fishing net. Marlin and Dory find Nemo.

**HINT** The numeral 1 has been placed in the correct picture for you.

**76**   **77**

## Fill In the Blanks

During a big storm, Prince Eric falls overboard. Read the text about storms. Then fill in the blanks.

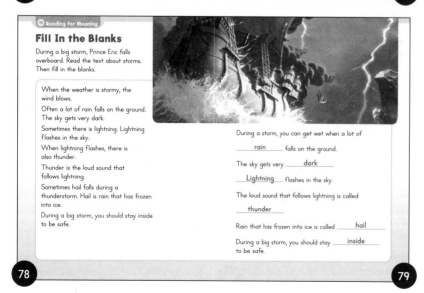

When the weather is stormy, the wind blows.

Often a lot of rain falls on the ground. The sky gets very dark.

Sometimes there is lightning. Lightning flashes in the sky.

When lightning flashes, there is also thunder.

Thunder is the loud sound that follows lightning.

Sometimes hail falls during a thunderstorm. Hail is rain that has frozen into ice.

During a big storm, you should stay inside to be safe.

During a storm, you can get wet when a lot of _____**rain**_____ falls on the ground.

The sky gets very _____**dark**_____

_____**Lightning**_____ flashes in the sky.

The loud sound that follows lightning is called _____**thunder**_____

Rain that has frozen into ice is called _____**hail**_____

During a big storm, you should stay _____**inside**_____ to be safe.

**78**   **79**

## Out of Order

Nemo has many friends. Read the words about Nemo's friends. Put the words in the right order.

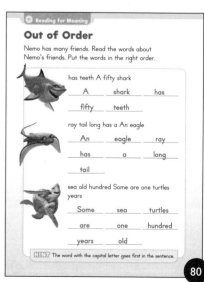

has teeth A fifty shark

_____**A**_____ _____**shark**_____ _____**has**_____
_____**fifty**_____ _____**teeth**_____

ray tail long has a An eagle

_____**An**_____ _____**eagle**_____ _____**ray**_____
_____**has**_____ _____**a**_____ _____**long**_____
_____**tail**_____

sea old hundred Some are one turtles years

_____**Some**_____ _____**sea**_____ _____**turtles**_____
_____**are**_____ _____**one**_____ _____**hundred**_____
_____**years**_____ _____**old**_____

**HINT** The word with the capital letter goes first in the sentence.

**80**

*Sample answers provided.

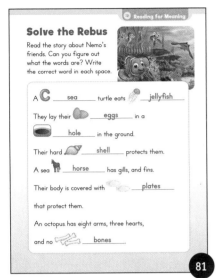

## Solve the Rebus

Read the story about Nemo's friends. Can you figure out what the words are? Write the correct word in each space.

A C___ __sea__ turtle eats __jellyfish__

They lay their __eggs__ in a __hole__ in the ground.

Their hard __shell__ protects them.

A sea __horse__ has gills, and fins.

Their body is covered with __plates__ that protect them.

An octopus has eight arms, three hearts, and no __bones__

81

**Word Bank**

happy   sad   walk   wish   human   dance

Ariel is __sad__ because she lives under the sea.

Ariel wants legs so she can __dance__ and __walk__

Ariel gets her __wish__

Ariel becomes __human__

Ariel is __happy__ she will live in the human world.

83

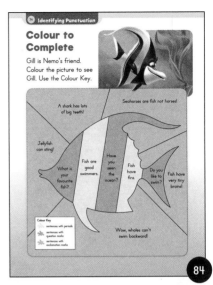

## Colour to Complete

Gill is Nemo's friend. Colour the picture to see Gill. Use the Colour Key.

A shark has lots of big teeth!

Seahorses are fish not horses!

Jellyfish can sting!

What is your favourite fish?

Fish are good swimmers.

Have you seen the ocean?

Fish have fins.

Do you like to swim?

Fish have very tiny brains!

**Colour Key**
- sentences with periods
- sentences with question marks
- sentences with exclamation marks

Wow, whales can't swim backward!

84

## Fill In the Blanks

What are Nemo and Crush doing? Complete each sentence with a period or an exclamation mark to find out.

**Punctuation**
.   !

Nemo and Crush are having fun __.__

They are swimming in the ocean __.__

Here comes a big wave __!__

They can ride the wave __.__

Hooray __!__

They did it __.__

They can ride the next wave, too __.__

Riding waves is so much fun __!__

85

## Maze

Sebastian is late for the concert. Find the correct path to help him find the way. Look for the sentence with the correct capitalization.

What music do you like   sebastian is late.

The concert is soon   Will Ariel be there?

86

## Fill In the Blanks

Ariel lives under the sea! Learn more about Ariel. Fill in the blanks with the missing pronouns.

**Word Bank**

they   you   He
Her   She   It

Ariel is a mermaid.

__She__ loves adventure.

__Her__ friend is Flounder.

__He__ is a guppy.

Together, __they__ explore the ocean.

__It__ is a lot of fun.

Do __you__ like to go exploring?

**HINT** Some of the words start with capital letters.

87

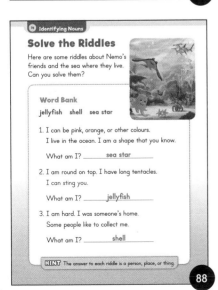

## Solve the Riddles

Here are some riddles about Nemo's friends and the sea where they live. Can you solve them?

**Word Bank**

jellyfish   shell   sea star

1. I can be pink, orange, or other colours.
   I live in the ocean. I am a shape that you know.

   What am I? __sea star__

2. I am round on top. I have long tentacles.
   I can sting you.

   What am I? __jellyfish__

3. I am hard. I was someone's home.
   Some people like to collect me.

   What am I? __shell__

**HINT** The answer to each riddle is a person, place, or thing.

88

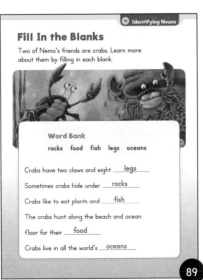

## Fill In the Blanks

Two of Nemo's friends are crabs. Learn more about them by filling in each blank.

**Word Bank**

rocks   food   fish   legs   oceans

Crabs have two claws and eight __legs__

Sometimes crabs hide under __rocks__

Crabs like to eat plants and __fish__

The crabs hunt along the beach and ocean floor for their __food__

Crabs live in all the world's __oceans__

89

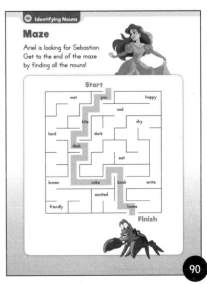

## Maze

Ariel is looking for Sebastian. Get to the end of the maze by finding all the nouns!

**Start**

wet   pan   happy

sad

little   dark   dry

hard

desk

eat

brown   cake   book   write

excited

friendly

home

**Finish**

90

*Sample answers provided.

**109**

# Answers

### Word Search

Ariel wants to be a part of the human world. What does she want to do when she gets there? Complete the word search to find out.

| S | T | R | O | L | L | M | R |
|---|---|---|---|---|---|---|---|
| J | T | W | R | U | N | K | T |
| A | Y | P | S | T | J | K | J |
| D | A | N | C | E | B | S | N |
| A | T | R | C | X | T | L | W |
| I | S | T | A | N | D | R | A |
| S | J | E | G | C | N | R | L |
| J | U | M | P | J | D | D | K |

DANCE
JUMP
RUN
STAND
STROLL
WALK

**91**

### Solve the Riddles

Nemo and his friends can do many different things. Read the clues and write what each can do!

**Word Bank**

fly   swim   read

1. Nemo lives under water.
   Nemo uses fins to move.

   Nemo can ___swim___!

2. Dory looks at words.
   Dory knows what they mean.

   Dory can ___read___!

3. Nigel flaps his wings.
   Nigel soars through the sky.

   Nigel can ___fly___!

**92**

### Fill In the Blanks

There are lots of fun fish in the ocean. Learn more about them. Fill in the correct adjective.

**Word Bank**

yellow   hard   pointy   white

Mr. Ray has ___white___ spots.

Dory has a ___yellow___ tail.

Crush has a ___hard___ shell.

Bruce has ___pointy___ teeth.

**93**

### Solve the Riddles

Ariel goes on many adventures in the ocean. Learn more about Ariel! Circle the correct adjective to solve the riddle!

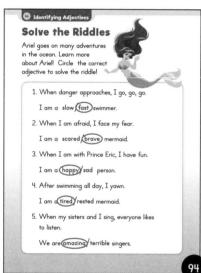

1. When danger approaches, I go, go, go.

   I am a slow (fast) swimmer.

2. When I am afraid, I face my fear.

   I am a scared (brave) mermaid.

3. When I am with Prince Eric, I have fun.

   I am a (happy) sad person.

4. After swimming all day, I yawn.

   I am a (tired) rested mermaid.

5. When my sisters and I sing, everyone likes to listen.

   We are (amazing) terrible singers.

**94**

### Fill In the Blanks

Ariel signs the contract Ursula gives her. A contract is a promise that is written down. Fill in each blank and make your own contract!

I promise to ___ *help at home

I will also ___ *be a good friend

I will not ___ *be unkind

Signed,

___
your name

**95**

### Unscramble the Words

Read the story. Unscramble the words in the story so the story makes sense.

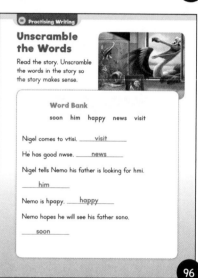

**Word Bank**

soon   him   happy   news   visit

Nigel comes to vtisi. ___visit___

He has good nwse. ___news___

Nigel tells Nemo his father is looking for hmi.

___him___

Nemo is hpapy. ___happy___

Nemo hopes he will see his father sono.

___soon___

**96**

### Solve the Riddle

Squirt and Nemo like to play a game. Read the poem about their game. Solve the riddle to find out what game they like to play.

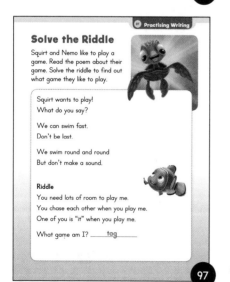

Squirt wants to play!
What do you say?

We can swim fast.
Don't be last.

We swim round and round
But don't make a sound.

**Riddle**

You need lots of room to play me.
You chase each other when you play me.
One of you is "it" when you play me.

What game am I? ___tag___

**97**

### Picture Search

Look at the picture. Who is in the picture? What is happening? Write a sentence about this picture.

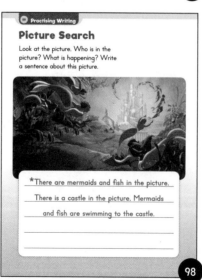

*There are mermaids and fish in the picture. There is a castle in the picture. Mermaids and fish are swimming to the castle.

**98**

### Fill In the Blanks

Imagine Ariel needs help to finish this letter to Sir Grimsby. Fill in the blanks with the missing words.

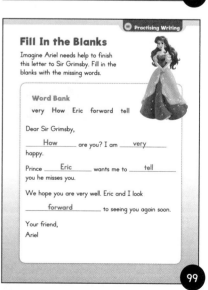

**Word Bank**

very   How   Eric   forward   tell

Dear Sir Grimsby,

___How___ are you? I am ___very___ happy.

Prince ___Eric___ wants me to ___tell___ you he misses you.

We hope you are very well. Eric and I look ___forward___ to seeing you again soon.

Your friend,
Ariel

**99**

**110**

*Sample answers provided.

Cut out these flash cards. Use them to practise reading and writing.

-ag

-un

-et

-ug

-op

-ig

-at

-en

-ip

bet get jet let
met net pet
set wet yet

bun fun nun
run sun

bag gag lag
nag rag sag
tag wag

big dig fig
pig rig wig

cop hop mop
pop top

bug dug hug
jug mug rug
tug

dip hip lip
rip sip tip

den hen
men pen ten

bat cat hat
mat pat rat
sat

Cut out these flash cards. Use them to practise reading and writing.

Cut out these flash cards. Use them to practise reading and writing.

| | | |
|---|---|---|
| fast | cold | small |
| tall | up | soft |
| in | day | happy |

out

short

slow

night

down

hot

sad

hard

big

Cut out these flash cards. Use them to practise reading and writing.

Cut out these flash cards. Use them to practise reading and writing.

dark

wet

good

high

empty

above

.

i

?

bad

dry

light

below

full

low

Say a sentence. Ask your child
to pick the correct punctuation
from the three cards.

Say a sentence. Ask your child
to pick the correct punctuation
from the three cards.

Say a sentence. Ask your child
to pick the correct punctuation
from the three cards.

Cut out these flash cards. Use them to practise reading and writing.

# Congratulations

_____!

Print your name.

You have finished the
Brain Boost learning path.
Way to go!